One Rupee Film Diaries: A Theory of Every Being

(Part 2)

ANAMITRA ROY

DEDICATION

Khakee,
The street-dog
Who spent life as a pet
To Sriparna and left
Us in 2008

CONTENTS

ACKNOWLEDGMENTS

Members and supporters of Little Fish Eat Big Fish, our no-budget filmmakers' forum, without you this book won't have been possible! Thanks a lot for being there in the time of need...

1 WHY THEORY

It's not arrogance. It's a kind of confidence that keeps on radiating when
you know what you are doing. If you take it as arrogance the only reason
behind this attitude of yours is probably the consumer's ego. The artists you
have known are mere puppets held above and promoted by merchants.
Those puppets don't have the rights to make a statement firmly until and
unless they are told to do so by their creators, that is, the merchants. They,
being politically incorrect, often brag about themselves and badmouth
about each other. Those egoistic doggings and bitchings maybe out of
arrogance or maybe these are just marketing efforts but you, quite easily, eat
that up as gossips, while, when people like us say something; it's the politics
inside us, the driving force that makes us work. With your reading-gossips-
in-a-newspaper-like-attitude, you really can't make anything out of it. So, all
you can see in the sentences is just the violent echo. You are so far away in
your galaxy made of the stock market and life insurance policies, you just
can't connect to core. On our part, yes, sometimes we do become arrogant.
It happens mostly when without any reason you allege us of arrogance. You
can't really imagine the situations we work in. Also, there's this sleep lack to
be blamed that makes us feel agitated. You may say that you are an IT
professional and you know what sleep lack feels like, but my friend, you are
doing that for money, or allow me to put it like this, out of your own greed
you are staying awake and working whereas we keep on working because
there is a purpose, we feel, greater than anything in the world. It's an urge
we feel day and night. Maybe we are from different worlds really. I mean,

who knows all the mysteries of this universe!

In the first volume of this diary, I consciously avoided mentioning these contradictions and tried to stay close to the facts. But this volume is about the theory which is of no use to most of you. Only people like us can make any sense out of it and put it to some work. So, if you could not connect to whatever I wrote above, proceed at your own risk.

Personally, I'm against theories, because theories are generalizations and generalizations are only half-truths. To study patterns, disciplines, orders, symmetries or series of similar events, they should be approached in two different ways,

    i)   Generalized
    ii)   Specialized

Now what we are talking about in this book is a generalized approach towards a specialized sector, that is, art in terms of communication. There are two faces of it; firstly, the way the artist communicates with the exterior verbally and secondly, the way the artist communicates through his or her art. These two angles contribute equally to the projection of an artist in whole in front of the audience. And this projection in its totality contributes to the factor how the art created by that certain person is going to be received in general. We shall come back here later.

From the very beginning of history, art has survived because it has either been appreciated as well as supported by the rulers or it has been appreciated and supported by the people. We live in a democracy, so to speak. So for us, in these changed times, reality is fragmented. There are rulers of course and they are identifiable. We see them everywhere, these rulers and the entertainers they promote in the name of artists. It's really easy to get, in fact, this one is the easiest part, but people or the community that should be supporting the real artists has become much dicey. Every individual is fragmented. They choose the rulers that suck their blood. So, there is a little fragment of the ruler too in every individual. For urban societies, the binaries like classic versus folk does not work anymore. With the democratization, the age of the great artists is now gone. There are no more great artists or unquestionable genii. Everyone is under microscopic analysis of the intelligentsia as well as the half-literates. This is democracy, you cannot tell anyone that your art is not for everyone or something like that. Those statements might make you sound like an 'elitist' which makes you politically incorrect to the 'people'. When you make your piece of hard work available, you cannot really control who reads it or watches it or writes a review in some newspaper. So, you better make it either really lucid so that everyone who comes across it understands everything or you should make it so different and difficult that people, whom you don't want to make a statement about it, starts feeling alienated within the first five minutes of coming across it. Or you might like to make it double layered in a way that people who are looking for some food-for-thought sees the inner layer and people who are unable to see it also enjoys your work in and out.

These are just thoughts. They just came to my mind when I was in search of something universal – a language, a logic system that works in this ultra-corporate world full of carpetbaggers. We need to know our audience in all its varieties. Learning what human beings are all about; that's the first step of becoming an artist, isn't it - to see the contradictions and conflicts in work and depict them in such a way that it conveys what you want to express.

Culturally, crowd-funding is not something new and neither did it come into existence after the launch of websites like *Kickstarter*. All the countries are run by crowd-funding only. Taxes, as you know it, are basically donations to a purpose, that is to say, you are contributing your money to a cause, the cause of social welfare or the cause of services or facilities that you think should be available in the society. Even when the world was run by kings, people used to pay taxes so that the king remains able to save them from the hands of invaders by maintaining an army. Church also does live on donations made by human beings. Historically, there are plenty of examples of crowd-funding. It's really not that new as it seems to be. It is natural that a community of people conscious about their right to culture would participate in producing their own cultural products. Now let's come to crowd-funding in films. Ritwik Ghatak's *Nagarik (1952)* was a co-operative effort or Satyajit Ray did ask for credit from people he knew while making *Pather Panchali (1955)*, but Shyam Benegal's *Manthan (1976)* is considered to be first crowd-funded film made in India. The next one we know about is *Amma Ariyan (1986)* by John Abraham. When it comes to the world, crowd-funding for films, as we know it today, was probably introduced by John Cassavetes while making his first feature film, *Shadows (1959)*. It was of course a path less traveled, but it was there. Platforms like *Kickstarter* or *Indiegogo* only made it popular.

There was I, with a microphone in my hand, standing with Sriparna, Twish and Gurpal on the evening of 25th February, 2012, appealing to people to chip in their hard earned money for a film we would like to make. It was going to be a film without stars, a film produced within much constraints, waging battle against limitations and lack of resources. Unfortunately enough, in a country like India, neither a documentary nor a fiction, it was going to be a docu-fiction, nevertheless, that too about independent filmmaking in India!

There was I, but why did I put myself there, to perform such a difficult task? One year later or so, I would have to write things like "why should you donate to the 0ne rupee film project?--- well, apparently there are no reasons why you should!" I knew it in advance, the complex reactions our launch was going to provoke. It was not supposed to be easy. We have seen self-proclaimed aspiring indie filmmakers who do not really have the idea that a short film is not necessarily a documentary or a fiction film is not necessarily a feature. We have seen hobbyist filmmakers calling themselves indies. We have seen amateurs claiming to be the real guys who belong to the underground. We have seen awkwardly Bollywood-ish film being promoted and accepted as a path-breaking indie film. We have seen 'seniors', how ferocious they can become when they start feeling that a kid they met yesterday and provided some useless advices to might become a bigger name than them tomorrow (when you only care about how to get grants you often end up making insignificant films and once you realize how insignificant your works are it's natural for you to feel unsafe)!
We were in this country and we were using terms people talk about because it seems cool but they don't really care about. What else was there to expect? Yet one has to make decisions. What made me took that decision? How did I analyze the situation, or, in other words, what was my theory?

Certainly, there was one; my blue print of how to serve the greater purpose. As I had said in the previous volume of this series, maybe someone is actually reading this diary (some people did in case of the previous volume), but as a DIY artiste I have no illusions, may be no one will read this diary ever. So, the sole purpose of writing comes back to the same; rediscovery of the self. We went through a lot of inner conflicts. I'll try to introduce a structure to all that was taking place in our minds before and after taking that one giant leap.

To be or not to be, if that is the question we did choose to project, to play, to perform!

And thus, eventually, to become!

2 WHAT THEORY

Why am I doing this to myself? I really don't know why I have to do this every time or why I cannot do anything else. I know where I could be and wherever I am I chose it by myself. It was my decision. I became what I wanted to be, not driven by circumstances at all. Always, I took the decision being completely aware that we become what we do. So, no one or nothing is there to be blamed. And I'm doing it again. Even this book is not some commercial writing. I'm just talking to myself which would be of interest to no one I suppose. Commercial writings are not like this, I know. I could have used these diaries to raise funds for the completion of our film. I could have filled these with my opinion about interesting people in the industry, I mean people, people like to hear about or people who can be sold over and over again, like celebrities or industry stalwarts. But no, it's just I'm talking to myself trying to discover how I came this way.

It's the natural process of excretion. It's how it has always been for this introvert kid who seems arrogant at times. A good thing about writing a book is, when you are writing there's no one around to disturb you. No one is trying to bend you or make you stoop before their consumerist ego! I know consumers always have to say the ultimate thing about a product. But they don't know that their desires are not their own desires. There's a radio-active network in place to tell them what to desire. This is something some people seem to be unaware of. They don't even believe that there really can be someone who just doesn't give a damn about the market. An artiste, for them, is someone who makes cultural products for sale. They have no idea that it can be something like breathing for someone, a part of life, that is to say, you cannot live healthily without.

Have you heard someone writing a book like naming the chapter anything and then writing just anything that seems to go with the name? Of course, he is writing his diary. He doesn't have to deliver a thriller with a plot to entertain you. Entertainment you always get and that's what makes you numb. In today's world you are supposed to go with the flow. You are not supposed to think. Even when you are driving you are supposed to turn on the music. If it's a radio channel being aired they'll surely play something zingoistic, some popular mindless stuff and you'll think, wow, you're enjoying life! Well, are you enjoying really, you stuck in the horrible traffic of Bangalore, Mumbai, Delhi or Kolkata? Or even in New York? I don't know, I think I got a problem here. I don't find peace in your so called development. Something keeps on ticking inside my head and the head feels heavier (like a box full of explosives)!

I had to talk too much during the last couple of years. I had to hide myself and act as a fundraiser-filmmaker. So, this was important, to get naked, stand in front of the mirror to locate the hypocrisies and admit. Only after knowing where I stand I'll be able to move forward.

There was I, in search of the universal thing. There was never a lack of idea for us. But money, that was something we really did lack. Firstly, the whole no-budget chapter, that is to say, Little Fish Eat Big Fish and the 3 DVDs, my paper aimed at defining no-budget film; it was all part of the same plan. It was all political activism for me. I come from a left liberal background, you know, Jean Paul Sartre and all that. For me the world was a playground for self-developed games. I was always this kind of an idiot. I would fight for Tagore or even Bhagavad Geeta with the Marxists and I would gift Hungry Generation literature on birthday of a friend who never read anything else but Tagore. Thesis-antithesis-synthesis, that was the ultimate truth for me. The popular story of D.G Phalke founding the Indian film industry, if we go by that, he was inspired by nothing else but the European film industry. We have heard the story of Phalke watching Life of Christ in 1910 and envisioning the Indian gods on screen etc several times. He did Indianize cinema by turning the mythological stories into films, but the India I saw after birth was hugely a different one. Now, Phalke used to work for Raja Ravi Verma. Just for the people unaware of these facts, this Raja is a painter who contributed the most in building up the popular visual culture of India. He gave the inseparable faces, that we see today, to our gods. So, it was natural for Phalke to remain limited in mythology considering the background he comes from. Filmmaking is a rich man's thing. It was only similar to what was going on all over the world during those days. Even when double-bills were already introduced in America and the poverty-row studios came into existence, in India it was still a rich man's thing mostly. One of the biggest stars of that era was P.C Barua who belonged to a Zamindar family of Assam, related to the royal family of Cooch Behar and B. N Sircar was the son of the then advocate-general of Bengal. Making a film surely meant spending a hell lot of money. Thanks to digital technology that in the 21st century we can think to give it a try at least. The background we come from (discussed in volume 1 already), has made us see people from both sides of the margin because we are on the margin itself. We have met people making money in the name of making films as well as people wasting money or turning black money into white through the means of making films. We have also known people who can never even think of thinking about making a film. We have spent days with people who want to make films but have no means. We have talked to people who made a film when they were younger and now struggling to earn a living or find a roof. We have seen once-upon-a-time-made-a-documentary-and-won-a-couple-of-awards filmmaker suffering from cancer and having no money to get admitted to the hospital. What makes them come this way?

There was I, looking for a way, on which we can meet all of these guys and say hello comfortably, a logic that has the power to provide answer to people from any segment of the society. I felt I was answerable to something, if not someone. The greater purpose, the people who served the same, I felt, and I still do feel, are my homies. But the language of my home is not understood by everyone. So, I needed a language that, maybe in a different way, but foreigners would understand as well as my homies.

Crowd-funding, it is closely related to the hysteric conception we call people's art; it is also closely related to market resource management. It is a radical way of gathering money for your film, yet it's a trendy thing that I felt, was going to become too popular too soon. The One Rupee Film Project, the concept here allows everyone to take part in producing a film by contributing as minimum as USD 0.017 $. It is related to radical democratization of the concerned medium where no class or caste barriers can stop one who wishes to stand by a film he or she feels for. It is related to building up a database of people interested in off-the-track filmmaking and eventually forming a community to support these kinds of efforts. But, nevertheless, it is related to micro-finance also. In pure words, it was a stunt to get attention from a lot of people and thus building up an audience for the kind of films that we make.

We are writers, poets, painters. Creative independence is our thing. We never compromised or surrendered to the demands of the market. We never let anyone alter our visions just because he or she could make us popular and rich within six months or so. We felt that language was becoming a barrier for whatever we create. That was the primary reason we decided to make films for. Also, the film industry, since more than two decades, was just producing trash. After watching good films and the range of varieties like from John Ford to Woody Allen or from Fellini to Tornatore, I mean, let's not go to the names because there's no end to the list even if only Europe and America is considered. Then there's this whole new world of Iran. These are what made us kick so hard that we could not tolerate whatever was going on in the name of cinema in West Bengal, India in 2008-2009. So we founded the forum. Another reason was lack of money of course. Since we had firsthand idea of the costs related to digital filmmaking we became really interested to develop a new aesthetics of money-less cinema. Dogme '95 imposed limitations on itself for sake of a new aesthetics and in our case the limitation was already there. What we needed was more intelligent interpretation of our limitations. Now, in the post-digital era, Little Fish Eat Big Fish was the first no-budget filmmakers' collaborative in India, also the first indie filmmakers' collaborative in the country. The first direct to DVD release of indie films in India was too executed by us. In 2011, all of a sudden, the scenario changed. Indie became the new hotcake and pandemonium began. Everyone is suddenly an independent filmmaker. By everyone, I indicate to two categories mainly. Firstly, the people who were never interested in poetry, literature, painting or theater or even Cinema or any other art form, secondly, people serving and using casts and set-ups of the mainstream film industry and also catering to a certain market or niche pre-defined by the industry; all of them suddenly started claiming to be independent filmmakers. Also, another phenomenon (yes, phenomenon) did took place in 2011. Gandu, the film by Q, it was suddenly so popular that it became the face of radical indie films from Bengal (if not from India) and novices who were looking for fame and money started making bunch of short films on explicit themes as if that was the key to all their problems. Naturally, we had to do something to let people know that a different kind of indie films, politically enriched and matured, does exist in Bengal that refuses to submit to this new fever surrounding the "smart & cool stuff"!

Now where do we hit in this kind of a case?
To be precise, we hit in the face.
And that's how independent filmmaking itself became the subject of our docu-fiction. This fake indie-air, that has nothing to do with creative independence, needs to be cleared, not by opposing it or protesting against it, but by making them reveal what their intentions are or what impact they could create, and by juxtaposing it with the opposite, the real parallel that never cares about a tag and can go to any extent to save its Independence wildly!

3 THE BLACK HOLES

They are the stars, we are the black holes. It's really as simple as that. You discover them because you can see them. They glow in the night. We don't glow. The region we live in, does not let light come out of it, margin or the other side of the margin. Even when you discover us, it's because of them, just like in the case of the black holes. There are three general ways to detect a black hole in the sky. Firstly, you can detect one from the behavior of glowing matters surrounding or revolving around it. For instance, in our case, someday someone may find out one of these 250 (actually more than that) people who contributed or took part in our film and come to know about us from them. Maybe someday someone of this 250 would become a star and people would notice and come to know about our film from his or her filmography. Another way to detect a black hole is following a phenomenon known as the gravitational lens effect. Stars that are far away from earth sometimes seem to change their relative position for a limited period of time. It is said that a black hole must have been there between earth and that very star for that certain period of time and that's why its gravitational field has forced the light to bend making the star appear in a different position when observed from earth. In our case, a perfect example of gravitational lens effect would be if someday we get some celebrity endorsement. You'll think that the celebrity is honest at heart and devoted to the cause of better cinema as he or she supports unrecognized true independent filmmakers and this point-of-view of yours will change the coordinates of projection of that very celeb for a limited period of time. Black holes can be detected by observing x-ray radiations too. You see, when the black holes eat up stars, they get heated up and emit a large amount of x-ray from a certain place known as 'event horizon'. It's like when we talk about the celebs of your world or your Oscars etc., we do get heated up and use sarcasm or harsh criticism. This radiation sometimes makes us get noticed by a larger audience. For instance, a couple of months ago, an acquaintance of ours named Jesse Richards posted an open letter to Hollywood on the blog maintained by their filmmakers' (read black holes') collaborative. This letter caught my eye and I started taking Jesse seriously. A number of American black holes, pardon me, I mean, marginal filmmakers also signed under this letter agreeing with the statement. This event got them some attention for sure. I did include this phenomenon in an article I was writing then for a Bengali webzine. I'm writing about that here again. So, it can be said that this very event of emitting radiation has certainly increased the detectability of the black hole named Jesse Richards.

Can the subaltern speak, it was a great question to ask. For a moment, let's forget about subalterns. We are not subalterns, they belong to the other side of the margin. We are from the margin itself and the margin is not a small place, it's huge. But from what I see here, I would like to reverse the question. Actually, can the academician speak? We are speaking and we know, they are hearing. But, they are not speaking. They'll speak for sure if our film makes it big in the theaters or in the film festival circuit, or if we were academicians ourselves our colleagues would have, even if the film was not this unique by nature. So, what conclusion does come out of it? Are they not allowed to speak? The publish-or-perish environment that they live in, has it imposed certain limitations on them? Since I was a student of Jadavpur university, I have seen acclaimed academicians. I have also known some of them personally. They spend a hell lot of words on anything, just anything (for self-amusement maybe), provided that the specimen or the samples belong to a safe cultural environment. By safe cultural environment, what I mean is, a structure that produces stuff which doesn't challenge or question the status quo. Hollywood is Hollywood, nouvelle vague is nouvelle vague, neo-realism is neo-realism and if it's an Indian film it must have been noticed and picked up by elite foreigners to be entered and discussed in the terrain of academics, or it must belong to a public acknowledged film industry. They just won't step out of their comfort zone to discover newer things by themselves. I mean, what's wrong with them! *Chinnamul (1950)* by Nimai Ghosh is the first neo-realist Bengali film. OK! Then why don't you show it to the students instead of De Sica, or along with De Sica may be! You never mentioned Barin Saha in any of the courses included in all the four semesters we had to clear in two years. Whatever you taught us, I can have all that information on the internet for free and also, I know how to buy books! What the hell is the purpose of the esteemed Film Studies Department of Jadavpur University if it doesn't introduce students to what already has been done here in our state or country. You never screened *Om Dar B Dar* by Kamal Swaroop or *Kalpana* by Uday Shankar but you taught us about New American Cinema

Group and American Underground Cinema. What's your problem? What are you waiting for? If you don't take the step, who is supposed to do that? When I was writing my dissertation on no-budget films, in the first sitting, I remember my mentor saying, "I'm not expecting advocacy for the Indian no-budget scene which has not properly flourished yet in your paper, you know, I'm kind of afraid since I know you and your friends have made a forum and you make no-budget films yourself"! I was not even thinking of something like that (probably due to the effect of the environment of our department) at that time, but today I ask you, dear sir, what am I supposed to do? Should I try and raise money to submit my film to Sundance and similar festivals, so that someday Mr. Tom Gunning writes about it and five years after that maybe you can allow someone to actually write a paper on the Indian no-budget scene? Getting awards abroad, is that what you mean by a flourished no-budget film movement; not a self-consuming and well organized sector?

Dear sir, would you please like to wake up?

This memory just helped me remember a recent incident. I was talking to a journalist about our film. He is the editor of the entertainment section of a well-known Bengali daily. He said, "so basically you made a structure where only the people who are producing the film are supposed to watch it. Without a proper distribution plan, I don't think it is of much significance or would be of public interest really. Crowd-funding, you see, English dailies have already written a lot about it. There's nothing left for us. There are two news angles that I can see; one is, if a celebrity backs your film or watches it and talks to the media, and the other one is the same old story of the struggle of independent filmmakers. Now it's your decision." I told him, "there's no need to go for the second one. Independent filmmaking is much more about slapping than crying or begging, I believe". I could have told him about Glauber Rocha and importance of a self-consuming structure in a film movement, but I didn't. After all, he is just an editor of an entertainment supplement, and also, we were talking for the first time. People get the leaders and celebs they deserve. Really!

Last year in December, a big guy, the head of the sound department of one of the most reputed film institutes in India, said, "you have taken off, this much can be said. It's not easy for fictions in this country. Had it been a documentary, it would have been much easier for you to get completion funds or to get a distribution deal. Now you are saying it's a docu-fiction. So, I don't know how much space you would get in the fiction field but you won't get accepted in the field of documentary for sure. You know what, you should have started with a documentary, everyone does that." This was in Chennai. An indies-only event was taking place there and they had called us to share our experiences. Later in the hotel room I was recapitulating what he said that evening. I felt happy to see that our idea did succeed to this extent that a big guy like him had to say that we have at least taken off. We made a forum, released DVDs, built up our own limited section of audience but we could not take off. After five years we finally could (in his eyes) and the credit goes to the 0ne rupee film project. This was part of the plan of course, to make guys like him take our initiatives seriously. At least now they'll admit, whatever we have made, irrespective of whether it finds a distribution deal or not, a film! So, after directing four short films that a limited number of people actually paid to watch and editing thirteen similar and also working with or making films for clients like National Union of Backward Classes or Jat Regiment of the Indian Army, finally, we have made our FIRST film!

Bravo!

From Chennai we went to Bangalore and then to Bhubaneswar and on the last but one day of the year, we were back in Kolkata. We showed the film to some of our friends during this trip. Some of them have worked in the film and some of them have not. They are from different backgrounds with different interests. Astonishingly, all of them found the film to be "Engaging" rather than entertaining or boring. Even more was waiting for us at Kolkata. Initially we were looking for completion funds because we wanted to do the audiography properly. We started trying at MIFF and waited till IFFI. By this time we got three offers of technical co-production; the first one from Jaipur, second one from Bangalore and the third one from a reputed studio in Mumbai. We could not accept these deals as we did not have money to take the whole team to a different city for dubbing. Also, we had no money left and during the fundraising campaign we had promised several rewards to the contributors. So, technical co-production was not the answer to all our problems. After returning to Kolkata, we started talking to people in the industry here (which we never did before). Some of them were interested to watch the film. We uploaded a private screener which some of them did watch. Unbelievably, they too found it engaging and intellectual high-art stuff. Though they did not agree to provide completion funds as they already know (and said as well) releasing this kind of a film in the theaters would result into sure financial loss, they promised us to provide support otherwise. They showed respect to the merit of the film, in Mumbai as well as in Kolkata, but we are yet to get completion funds! Four agencies have promised us that they will look into the prospects of international sales once the film is complete. But it's just not coming to meet in the middle. After all these, we are still chasing and still trying everything we can. I seriously don't know what to say! Maybe someday someone will provide the funds needed, maybe we won't get funds ever and this film would turn into a legend that no one has ever watched, maybe we will have to launch another frustrating fundraising campaign; sincerely, I don't know!

So, there was I, looking for a way, and here I am, looking for another. In between, seven hundred and sixty eight days have passed. We thought, the recipients deconstruct the text. So, we tried to know the recipient and build the text accordingly. But every year the world changes and it has been more than two years. After *Gandu*, we have got *Ship of Theseus* and *Lucia* which were not there when we began. If it's a good independent film, along with or apart from winning awards in festivals in Europe and America, people now expect celebrity endorsement or great run at the theaters. With more and more fake indies, indies without an urge to discover something new in terms of aesthetics and indies produced by the film industry, it has become lot more tougher than it was to make a film with a shoestring budget and get attention of a larger audience due to the merit of the idea, the concept or the film itself.

God knows where we are headed!

ABOUT THE AUTHOR

Anamitra Roy is a writer-filmmaker based in Kolkata, West Bengal, India. He has been one of the co-founders as well as the curator of Little Fish Eat Big Fish, the no-budget filmmakers' collaborative. Born in 1988, Roy started making his first independent short film in 2007 with Sriparna, his wife, soul-mate and co-activist. His only collection of Bengali poems, "Shabdoprokriyakoron", came out in 2008. Till date he has four shorts to his credit and a crowd-funded feature, Aashmani Jawaharat (popularly known as the One Rupee Film Project) as a director and more than a dozen as an editor. He obtained master degree in film studies from Jadavpur University in 2010. For other books by this author, visit http://www.amazon.com/author/royanamitra

Provide your personal feedback to anamitra629@gmail.com